The Christ
Shepherd of Loving Kindness

By David O'Malley
Dedicated to my parents,
Frances and Paddy
and to all parents
– the first teachers
of loving kindness.

Graphics by Val O'Brien

ISBN 978-0-9548388-7-4

©Don Bosco Publications 2007
Thornleigh House
Sharples Park
BOLTON BL1 6PQ
www.don-bosco-publications.co.uk

CONTENTS

INTRODUCTION

Most people who speak of *love* today tend to focus on the sensual and romantic love of novels and soap operas. That understanding of love has dominated lately, but it is only part of the story. The Greeks identified that type of love as *eros*, erotic love and it is one of a quartet of words that they used to describe love in its fullness. The other words they used were *storge* (family love), *philia* (friendship love) and *agape* (loving kindness). These aspects of love have been overshadowed by the emphasis in our culture on romantic and erotic love. In approaching the vocation of teaching this short book attempts to explore the practical implications of *agape*, loving kindness in the teaching role. There are no sharp distinctions between these four aspects of love and teachers will live all of them in different ways. However, the vocational nature of teaching awakens a more spiritual (agape) and self-sacrificing dimension of love that is best described today as *loving kindness.*

Loving kindness is a universal spiritual ideal. In Buddhism the concept is expressed as *metta*. In Islam the idea of loving kindness is expressed as a desiring for others what one would desire for oneself. In a similar way the Gospel asks us to love our neighbour as ourselves[1]. In the letters of St John, loving kindness is described as something in which we abide, a kind of presence in which we all live and that draws us into compassion and responsibility for one another. To love like this, is to be spiritual and to cross over into a mystery of common humanity that points beyond itself, to a deeper shared reality. In Christian language that reality is called *The*

---

1 Matthew 22:39

Kingdom of God, the place in which God is hidden in the ordinary; like buried treasure in a field.

Every teacher, working vocationally, in the field of education is looking for buried treasure. The teacher will unearth the strands of God's spirit that point to a loving presence at the heart of each person, hidden in relationships, and in the gifts among colleagues and pupils. In tantrums and in tragedies, in celebrations and shared silence, the same spirit of loving kindness will emerge, slipping into and out of focus in our poor spiritual sight. Now we see only dimly what will later become obvious; we need to work with the faith that God is with us. In the vocation to teach, we need a deeper insight to see that it is well worth going the extra mile.

This booklet is an attempt to sharpen the awareness of the teacher in recognising opportunities for loving kindness. It is reflective in style, so that experience and spirituality can combine into a personal knowing of the way that loving kindness emerges in the teacher's own life and style of working. It is an encouragement to contain negative emotions and take them into prayer. It will help teachers to support colleagues. It is an opportunity to recognise more clearly that there are moments for gratitude and celebration scattered throughout each day as teachers work with the young. This book is meant to be used to help evaluate that wider unspoken set of expectations that persist after the more measurable elements of teaching have been recorded and analysed.

Whilst the book is written from within a broad-based Christian tradition, it owes a large amount to the Salesian tradition of education pioneered by Saint John Bosco[2]. His emphasis on

---

2 See Appendix

loving kindness was the main focus of his *approach,* in helping very difficult youth in Turin in the mid-nineteenth century. He established a world-wide system of education which is practised in thousands of schools in over 125 different countries. His optimistic approach based on a broad Christian *humanism,* is one that is suited particularly to our western and secularised culture.

VOCATION

By nature and by grace,
You have been called to nurture the spirit of young people
In a world of crude measurements,
Of superficial images of success and celebrity.
You have been called into the personal mystery
Unfolding uniquely in the lives of each of your pupils.

You have been called to be a teacher
Not just to tick registers and write lists,
But to walk with young people,
On a shared journey into the heart of education.

On that journey you are both a leader and a learner.
Together with your pupils you will walk
The well-known paths of an academic year.
You will be surprised by the gifts, passions and problems,
Unfolding in the lives of the young.
For these children do not arrive empty-handed.
They carry the blessings and burdens of their short history.
Experiences of success and stability
Will sit alongside confusion and uncertainty,
In the heart of each member of your group.

How will you recognise the gifts among the grief,
In the silence of shy students?
How will you manage the noise of joy and jealousy,
Echoing in the exuberance and aggression of the young?
How will you sort the wheat from the chaff?
To break the bread of life, each day with them?

Only by embracing the wisdom of the spirit,
Will you feed their gifts and help them to grow.
Only by seeing with spiritual eyes,
Will you recognise and heal the hurt
That only loving kindness cures.

For your vocation is personal,
It is your personality that opens up
The ocean of goodness and strength in young lives.
It is only you who will engage
With one of these pupils in a way that sets them free.
Only you who might plant a seed, a hope or dream
That will burst into life in the hidden years yet to come.

You will be working in faith for a future not your own.
You will be nurturing potential that you cannot control.
You will be working with loving kindness,
For other people's children.

Your life will be poured out
In joy and generosity,
In patience and frustration,
Hour by hour, you will bear the heat of another day
Another term, another year.

You will be living a Gospel mystery:
For it is only when your life is poured out in love
Can you be filled with the utter fullness
Of the God for whom your life was made,
The God who has called you
To this vocation of teaching.

Reflection

What has teaching taught you so far?

What gifts have you discovered in your pupils?

Have you been able to encourage and guard the gifts of your pupils?

Where have you been able to create silence and stillness in your pupils?

How has your creativity, and ability to change, been developed?

When have you discovered the value of *wasting time* with pupils?

Which pupils leave you with a sense of frustration or worry?

With which colleagues do you feel a kindred vocational spirit?

How do you feel that your spirit has been sustained and inspired over the last week or term?

How far have family and friendships been a support or a victim of your vocation to teach?

After pouring life and energy into young lives, how will you rest awhile in the days ahead?

LOVING KINDNESS

Every spiritual tradition values loving kindness.
It sets up a deep connection between people,
Opening hearts and minds.
It gives you confidence with pupils and colleagues,
Sets free joy, warmth and genuine affection.

Working with loving kindness
Is an asceticism of the spirit for every teacher.
It is a discipline that becomes a way of life.
To be a teacher is not just a role but a rule for living
And sharing of life with the young in your care.

Loving kindness is an ideal that draws you
Deeper into the path of self-surrender,
Further into the mystery of that emptiness
Leading to a fuller life and to resurrection.

There is nothing soft or sentimental
About this path of loving kindness.
Loving kindness demands self-control
And self sacrifice.
It leads to strength of spirit and integrity,
It moves the focus from self to others.

Loving kindness is poured out in generous praise,
Celebrated in smiles of hospitality and humour.
It is expressed in balanced discipline,
in delicacy and respect.
Loving kindness builds up inner steel and spirit,
Comes to life, in the sacred space
between adults and young people.

Loving kindness recognises
that everything has been received,
As a gift to be given away.
Talents and troubles, goodness and grief,
Are all opportunities to exchange loving kindness,
To extend the network of life, among people.
As a shepherd of this loving kindness,

You are called to be ever alert
To the needs and the stories of the young,
Leading them, through celebrations and sadness
To deeper friendship and belonging.
Leading them to know the mystery of love,
Not far away, not as a fairy tale,
But as a lived experience now,
A love lived in friendship, in fun and forgiveness
Modelled in the life of their teacher every day.

Reflection

Who has touched your heart in kindness and compassion? Have you dealt with your own workload, your frailty and your life-balance with loving kindness?

Where have you seen loving kindness in young people? Have you had the opportunity to affirm and encourage that quality in them?

Where did you have an opportunity to affirm and encourage a colleague in their kindness and self-control under pressure?

Have you laughed and smiled enough?

Have you been able to challenge your pupils to generosity and self sacrifice?

When has someone recognised and named your own unspoken needs?

Where has your own heart been moved by the kindness and wisdom of your pupils?

Have you noticed any changes in the pattern of needs emerging in your pupils?

How have you been able to be a sign of Gospel love?

Discipline

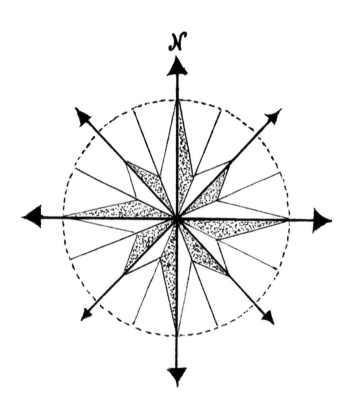

As a companion and guide for young people
You will need to avoid *the disease to please,*
The need to be liked and to be popular
Among the young people you lead.

Loving kindness means choosing life
Even when that choice makes you unpopular.
A leader who needs to be liked
Is a leader who is losing authority.

As a leader and guide you must be clear:
About rules - making them reasonable and consistent.
About options - making them obvious and balanced.
About consequences - always followed through.

True authority is rooted in genuine care.
It is expressed in honest affection and self sacrifice.
Young people will respect your authority
When you use reason and kindness.

Young people break rules because:
they are thoughtless,
they are testing your limits.
The first case demands that you remind, the second that you reprimand.
Both challenge you to build deeper trust through discipline.

Where there is no trust, rules become empty laws.
You become a prison officer.
Every breakdown in discipline is an opportunity
For the young to deepen their trust and grow in wisdom.
You can help young people take that chance to grow,
By the fair, consistent and caring way
With which you face their frailty, thoughtlessness and
immaturity.

Discipline maintained with loving kindness
Will make you a disciple of optimism
And new opportunities.
Each reprimand, made with kindness, at the right time,
Becomes a sign of respect and understanding,
Reinforcing the dignity of the young person
Despite their misdemeanour.

Each confrontation, faced by you as a teacher,
Tests the boundaries of your consistent care.
Each challenge to these limits,
Is also a challenge to your maturity.
The heart-felt struggle with poor behaviour
Transforms the one who disciplines, from a policeman
Into a disciple of loving kindness,
in the life of young people.

Reflection

In your decisions, words and body language, have you shown any favouritism?

Where have boundaries been broken by you or your pupils? Why did that happen and how did you manage the consequences?

Did you notice any times when pupils may have manipulated you through emotion, distraction or misinformation?

In reprimanding pupils have you been consistent and clear?

Have you followed up your threats in discipline, quickly and clearly?

Where have you been able to resolve discipline issues with a quiet word in the ear?

In reprimanding have you been able to avoid sarcasm or shouting?

Have you been able to maintain your self-discipline in punctuality, preparation and marking?

How well have you taken criticism and correction from your own colleagues and leaders?

Who among your colleagues have you been able to trust, to help you with discipline problems with pupils?

FORGIVENESS

The young people you teach
Need to see that you can be hurt,
And disappointed by their actions,
When they fall short of agreed standards.

There will be times when you will need
To withdraw affection and good humour
From young people whose behaviour
Has lacked dignity and respect.

Such coolness is an opportunity
For the young to take responsibility
For the way they have acted
And recognise that their teacher is a person
Whom they have the power to hurt.

You can forgive young people too quickly,
In a way that devalues the gravity of their behaviour.
They must recognise the damage they have done
To the trust that binds adults and young people.

You may need to deflect premature apologies,
With well-worked words and silences,
That say that you are too upset to talk.
Only when you sense this sadness and remorse,
Will your forgiveness lead to deeper trust.

Your forgiveness is a personal gift
to those who have gone astray.
It is not their right to assume you will give it automatically,
It must be earned through rebuilding
The shared partnership of learning for life.

Forgiveness is not a one-way street.
There will be times when you are wrong.
In actions, assumptions and judgements
You will make mistakes: you are only human.

There will be moments of deep education,
When you will need to ask your class for forgiveness
For what you have said or done,
Precious moments that reveal your dependence
Upon the goodness of the young people you serve.

There will be moments of peacemaking,
When you will hope and pray
That two young people will find the courage to forgive one another,
To let go of a bitterness that could last for years.

There will be times when you must forgive yourself,
For not being able to meet all the needs you recognise
In the faces of the young each day,
Especially at times of crisis and confusion.

You are only their teacher,
Not a saint, not a miracle-worker.
You are a servant of life and love.
Recognise when to hand over to God's wisdom,
The difficulties that are beyond your care.

Reflections

Which of your pupils needs to be forgiven by you?

Which pupils have saddened you?
How can you challenge them to make a new start?

Are there any colleagues that may need an apology from you?

Which pupils deserve an apology from you?

Who among your pupils would you like to bring to mutual forgiveness?

Are you in a position to ease the tensions and difficulties between any of your colleagues?

Is there any error of your judgement, or lapse in self-control, that you need to correct?

Can you forgive yourself for all the things you might have done if you had more time, more insight or more energy?

Are you ready to let this week or term go, with all its successes and failures, into the mystery of God's presence and trust His presence to give meaning to your struggle?

THE DUTY OF CARE

By virtue of your role as teacher,
You are in the front line of protection
And care for young people at risk.

It is you who will witness
The rhythms and patterns of young lives,
Played out in the routines of registration,
In the rough and tumble of school.

In healthy friendships and happiness,
And in their breakdown,
You will see the early signs of need
For care or confrontation.

With the parents of young people,
You will share a concern for each of your pupils,
To guide and correct, protect and encourage,
For the flourishing of their lives,
In laughter and friendship and hope for their future.

Care is part of the environment that you will build
In routines, in relationships and safeguards;
Creating a place of compassion and gentle honesty,
Within a wider crucible of joy and optimism.

The duty of care will become a common concern in class,
When you recognise compassion and kindness
Emerging in the life of your pupils.

Encouraging gifts of liveliness and understanding
Creates an atmosphere of hope and happiness.
It can embrace the fears of pupils who hide their hurt,
In silence or sarcasm in your class each day.

Care for your class will extend into discipline and delicacy.
The discipline of remembering birthdays,
The delicacy of a quiet word on an anniversary of
bereavement.
All speak of a warmth and care that changes you
Into a good shepherd, into a good teacher.

As a teacher you will also be on the receiving end
Of many silent blessings from the young
who know that you care,
But may never find the words to say so.
Their wordless thanks will leak out in awkward smiles,
Untroubled silences and lingering presence
at the end of class.
Read and cherish these tacit thank-you signs
That tell you that they know they have been heard,
Understood and cared for by you, their teacher.

Reflections

Where have you been able to express your care for pupils in need?

Where have you seen the most growth in pupils academically?

What changes in behaviour patterns among pupils cause you concern or give you hope?

How have you been able create a climate of care in the classroom?

What signs of physical and emotional deprivation have you observed?

How have you been able to recognise and quietly reward care and compassion among your pupils?

Where have you noticed tacit recognition for your care and concern for pupils?

Which colleagues have also shown some need for care and support?

How have you celebrated successes, birthdays, sadness and struggle in your pupils' lives?

How has the duty of care extended to your family, friends and yourself this term?

LOST SHEEP

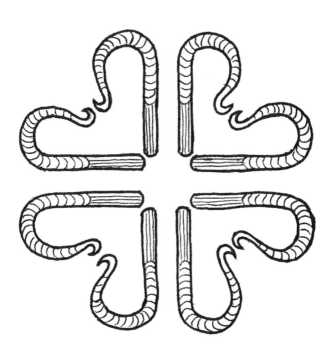

As a pastoral teacher you have been called,
Especially to the lost sheep.
The lost sheep may have disappeared,
Or shrunk and shrivelled into anonymity,
Hidden by the furniture and noise of the classroom.

As a shepherd of this group,
You are called to seek out the silent
And reconnect them with the group.
You are called to re-build the bridges,
Broken by anger and misunderstanding,
Leading home those who have been lost,
In bitterness and fear,
So that there will be just one flock
United around you, their shepherd.

As a shepherd, you are asked to be vigilant
For those who are being led astray.
To remind them of the rules, and of your care
Which holds them together.

It is much easier to bring home the lost
If they have not strayed too far.
Watch therefore, for destructive habits.
Distract, remind and challenge the flock,
To be the best they can be for each other.

Sheep will always follow a strong leader,
So try to build on the natural leaders
You will find among your pupils.
Encourage, guide and even train these young people
To be models of the kindness and example
To lead their companions to life.

When a young person changes their ways,
Avoids trouble, does well and joins in with the rest,
Celebrate the change and invite the class to rejoice.
Never lose a chance to recognise and reinforce their
goodness.

Never give up hope in the goodness
Of even the blackest of your sheep.
God did not crush the bruised reed
Or snuff out a wavering candle.
Let your model be the Good Shepherd
Who never gives up the search for the lost sheep.

Reflections

Which pupils have *you* tried to avoid?
Which of them will you need to seek out?

Who, among your pupils, needs a really good listening to?

Who is demanding too much of your attention by blatant behaviour that demands action?

How much do you know about the background of the lost sheep among your pupils?

Which pupils have shown promise of becoming leaders among their peers? Can you build their natural leadership into a positive gift, bringing the goodness out of all your pupils?

What other colleagues can speak effectively to the pupils who will not, for some reason, listen to you?
How can you use their better relationship to build trust with those pupils?

How have you celebrated any improvement in the behaviour of pupils?

Are there any pupils with whom you have given up hope?

Have you felt like a lost sheep?
What did you do about it?

COMMUNITY

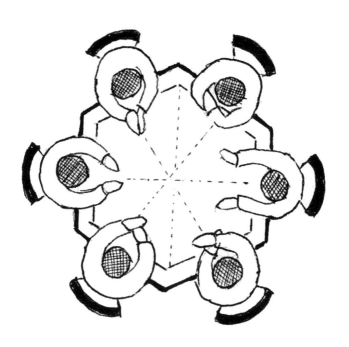

The class you meet each day in school
Is not a random group or an administrative unit.
It is above all a small community,
Within which young people can grow and flourish,
Or be put at risk and be diminished.

As the leader of this little community,
You will learn to feel and to recognise visibly
The growing pains and the aches of children,
As they move through adolescence.
This is a community of confusion and change,
Where identities are lost and found,
Where life ebbs and flows in relationships,
In the hopes and hormones of life.

This seething cauldron of community
Will bubble with energy and life
Generating a joy and spontaneity.
There will be sparks,
As unrealistic hopes, competition and emotion
Stir up minds and hearts that turn to you,
To make sense of what is happening.

As a community leader, you will be called upon
To earth the unrealistic expectations and angers
Of young adolescents, in your listening.
When you speak, you must look for words
That can turn experience into learning for life.
Words that will open their hearts to an understanding
That leads to personal insight and acceptance of others.
As a community leader of your children,
You will see the goodness of God,
Shining through the struggles of the young.
You will begin to see God as the foundation stone
Of your class and your community of life and love.

Wherever two or three are gathered, God is there.
Look therefore for the face of God in your pupils,
In all their moods, madness and meanings,
Your classroom is a *church*,
Where God's presence can be seen and named
By those who have the heart to look.

You, as leader in this little church,
Become their priest, the one who reveals
The hidden presence of God in the ordinary.
It is a priestly task to bless your group every day,
To take them by name into your private prayer,
To recognise the blessing they bring into your life,
As you share this little community and classroom church.

Reflections

Do pupils know and trust one another more or less than before?

Which pupils would you see as isolated and in need of inclusion?

What divisive issues are current among your pupils?
Can you make any difference to those issues?

How can you build bridges between the inevitable cliques?

How can you build your class groups into educating communities, where learning happens well in lessons and in life shared?

How have you celebrated the goodness in your pupils?

Where have you been able to connect community to the stillness, wonder and sacred mystery of the spirit in each person in the class? How has prayer been part of the class experience?

Where have you been able to name love in action among your pupils?

Where have you been able to challenge your classes, to move out in care for others in need and for the causes of justice and peace in a wider world?

How have you experienced colleagues as a community of care?
How have you been an active part of that care-giving this term?

LETTING GO

For better or for worse,
These precious and vulnerable young people
Will not be with you for very long.
They are not given to you for ever,
You will need to hand them on to others,
In hope and in faith for their future.

Let your parting be a sign of peace,
A celebration of all that you have shared.
Let their moving on become a party
That remembers the journey each one has made.

In memory boards and thank-you cards,
Let this milestone be a firm foundation,
From which they can move confidently into the future.

When possible, make moving-on
A personal thank-you for each pupil.
Each of them has received from you, but also given.
Whilst you have influenced each of them,
They too have given you new insights and experience.
You have been a blessing upon each other.
Even when you are relieved to see some pupils go,
They will remain a blessing in your memory.
In their struggle, they have tested your goodness,
Perhaps sent you to your knees in prayer,
When their needs exceeded your skill and strength.

In the end each one of them has been a gift.
The memory of your goodness
Will take your loving kindness into a future
You will never see.

When all is finished and they are gone,
Pray that the work you have done with them
Will be guarded and developed in God's wisdom
Let them go into that better world
That Christians call *The Kingdom of God*.

Reflections

How will you say goodbye to your pupils at the end of this year?

What kind of shared event will be most appropriate?

Which pupils will miss you the most as the year ends? Who will rejoice to see you move on?

What educational growth has the class achieved during the year? Has that been recognised and named clearly?

Are there any pupils that you may need to reassure of your continued care and prayers as you part company?

What have you learnt from this group of pupils?

How has teaching these pupils increased your sense of vocation and commitment to teaching?

How might your sense of vocation have been diminished this year?

How will you say goodbye to colleagues who are leaving at the end of this year?

What memories of the year come back to you with warmth and gratitude?

What memories of the year do you need to put into the hands of God as unfinished and confusing events and feelings in the year that is ending?

How will you now refresh yourself in mind, body, emotions and spirit?

A Saint's Advice

St John Bosco was an educator of young people in the city of Turin during the industrial revolution. Dealing with homeless and often damaged adolescents led to his development of *a preventive system*. This was based on a reasonable, affectionate and spiritual approach to the young. His approach worked with most young people and also helped the teachers to work with heartfelt realism for the good of young people. Here are a few of his thoughts on working with the young.

If I want to be a true Father to these children then I must have a Father's heart, and not turn to repression or to punishment without reason and without justice.

It is certainly easier to lose one's temper than to be patient; threaten young people rather than reason with them. It often suits our lack of patience and our pride to punish those who resist us, rather than bear with them firmly and with kindness.

Correction should be done in private and in an atmosphere of care for the individual. Never rebuke anyone in public except to prevent a disorder or to correct a disorder if it has already occurred.

I have rarely seen any advantage gained from improvised punishments inflicted before other means were tried.

Teachers do not always adopt the best approach in their dealings with young people. Either they hand out standardised punishments and achieve nothing, or they just strike out, rightly or wrongly. This is the reason why we often see disruption multiply and discontent spreading even among the better children.

If young people are already ruined at such an early age it is due more to carelessness than to any ingrained malice. These young people truly have a need for some kind person to show care, to work with them and guide them in virtues.

Let it be seen that no other rules are required than those that are absolutely reasonable and necessary.

Look for someone to whom the child can open up his troubles, in a way that perhaps he cannot do with you, because he is not sure that he will be believed, or because he is too proud to admit that he should.

When you have won over a stubborn spirit in a child I beg you not only to leave him the hope of being forgiven by you, but through good behaviour, to cancel even the memory of his mistakes.

To forget and to cause to be forgotten the unhappy days of a young person's mistakes, is the supreme art of a good educator.

You can get further with a friendly look, with a word of encouragement that gives new heart and courage, than you can with repeated blame which serves only to upset and diminish enthusiasm.

Teachers should try to avoid like the plague every kind of morbid affection or any exclusive friendship with any pupils. They should realise that the wrong doing of any one member of staff can compromise the whole institution.

Teachers should precede pupils to their class; they should remain with them until another teacher comes; they should never allow young people to be idle.

I have often noted that staff who demand silence, hand out punishments easily, and exacted prompt and blind obedience were invariably the ones who showed little respect for the useful advice that I and other colleagues found it necessary to give.

Teachers who never forgive their pupils are often in the habit of forgiving themselves everything.

Whenever there is a need to punish, great prudence is required. First of all wait until you are in control of yourself; do not let it be understood that you are acting because of a bad mood, or in anger. In this event you put your own authority at risk and the punishment would become harmful. Even the young realise that only reason has the right to correct them.

Do not punish anyone the moment that the fault has been committed, for fear that they may not be able to own up or to overcome their emotions and recognise the need for the punishment. Otherwise they may become even more embittered and commit the same or even worse faults. You need to give them time to recover, think things over and to acknowledge their mistakes. At the same time they are more likely to see the justice of the penalty imposed and so profit by the experience.

When teachers are thought of as superior and no longer as a Father figure or a friend: they are feared and little loved. And so, if you want to be of one heart and mind, for the love of God, you must break down this fatal barrier of mistrust and a replace it with a spirit of confidence. How do you break through this barrier? By a friendly and an informal approach with the young, especially in recreation. You cannot have loving kindness without this familiarity, and where it is not evident there can be no confidence. If you want to be loved you must make it clear that you love.

The more you act from spite, the less you will be listened to.

Let us rid ourselves of all anger when we have to curb young people's faults. No commotion of spirit, no scornful looks, no hurtful words on our lips. Instead, let us feel compassion for what is happening and offer hope for the future.

Let us remember that force punishes the offence but does not heal the offender. One does not cultivate a plant by harsh violence and so one does not educate the young person's will by burdening it with a yolk that is too heavy to bear.

Do not use expressions calculated to humiliate. Express hope and your readiness to forgive when the behaviour improves.

The teacher who is seen only in the classroom remains just another teacher and nothing more; but if they appear in recreation they become a friend. How many changes of heart have been achieved because of a quiet word in the ear whilst a young person is in recreation!

Someone who knows that they are loved will love in return, and one who loves can obtain anything, especially from the young.

Confidence creates an electric current between youngsters and their teachers. Hearts are opened, needs and weaknesses made known. This confidence enables the teacher to put up with the weariness, annoyance, the ingratitude and the troubles that young people cause. Jesus did not crush the bruised reed nor quench the wavering candle. He is your model. When this confidence and loving kindness fails nothing will go well.

Why do people want to replace loving kindness with cold rules?

Remember that education is largely a matter of the heart. The heart of a young person is like a fortress which is always closed to rigour and harshness. Let us strive to make ourselves loved. Then we will see the doors of many hearts open with great ease. God is the master educator and we will be unable to achieve any lasting good unless God teaches us the art of education puts the key into our hands

Prayers

Prayer after a Good Day

Lord, thank you for the goodness of today,
for the majority of young people
who are interested and no trouble.
Thank you for colleagues to trust
and teams that really work.

On days like these, I know why I became a teacher;
I can feel the gifts and the fulfilment
of this privileged role.
It is easy to see the goodness shining out of young lives,
Easy to see the hope and energy
moving in corridors and classrooms.

Help me to treasure these days
and remember how I feel tonight.
Today I see clearly, make connections and recognise gifts.
May the memory of this day sustain me
when I don't see as clearly.

The Fathers of the Church said - *when in desolation
remember consolation.*
Let this day be filed under consolation
to keep me going at other times.

May I always remember that I am always doing good,
Even when I do not see it clearly.
Most of what I do is hidden in the hearts of the young
Clouded over by hurry, darkened with disruption.
Today those clouds parted for a while.
I can see the goodness of my work
Breaking through an ordinary day.

Prayer after a Bad Day

Lord, it's been one of those days,
when nothing seems to work well,
I'm including pupils and staff!
Someone is setting a harsh climate in the school
I have made heavy weather of everything today.

Lord, help me to remember
that I am working with young people,
The most turbulent and stormy section of society.
They leak an unstable energy that can upset and inspire at
the same time.
This heady mix creates a climate of change that makes this
work
Fascinating but frustrating, today mainly frustrating.

Remind me Lord, that I am not responsible today
For this stormy upsetting atmosphere around the school.
It is in the nature of young people
to argue and to challenge adults.
Unpredictability is part of the vocation of teaching,
Riding the storms of days like these is part of the art of
survival.

The sailor does not blame the sea for the storms,
He adjusts the sails and takes a new tack in troubled waters.
The teacher too, needs to adjust expectations
of what is achievable
In the dips and swells of adolescent classrooms.

Today has been stormy, tempers have been frayed.
Tomorrow is a new day and another weather system,
Waiting to be navigated to new knowledge and experience.

Lord of sea and storm, be with me tonight,
Help me rest after the tensions of the day,
To call on your presence in the storms that threaten peace,
In school corridors and in my own heart tonight.

Prayer for Colleagues

Lord, I've crossed the path of many colleagues today.
I'm wondering what impression I have made.
Did I leave them happier, supported and understood?
Did I add to their burdens, reinforce their prejudices,
Or keep their kindness for me at arms length?

Lord, I know that teachers need to work together,
Even though we teach in separate classrooms.
I know I need colleagues to be consistent in discipline,
If my discipline is to make sense to pupils.
I need other teachers to leave classes calm and focussed,
If I am to get through the next lesson with them.

I need colleagues who have time to listen
To the issues and problems of my work.
I need friendly colleagues who can laugh
And talk about anything but teaching.

I know that I need all those things and more,
So what kind of a friend have I been to colleagues today?
How have I played my part in the team,
Supported the weak and encouraged commitment?

Lord, make me a good friend to colleagues.
Help me to see your loving kindness in each of them
However deeply they may have hidden it.
Help my smile and kindness awaken in their hearts
Your own presence within them, for their lasting good.

Prayer for Pupils

Lord it would break my heart if I let it.
There is so much unspoken suffering in young lives
In the classes I have taught today.

Part of me just doesn't want to know
But occasionally I get a glimpse of home situations,
That leave me with a mix of tears and admiration
For the resilience of the young.

My own subject seems to fade into the background
Before such huge emotional burdens
Set across the shoulders of children
Who quietly act out a love that asks too much.

How far do I get drawn into these needs, Lord?
Where does my job end?
Do I let them off with poor behaviour or with late work?
How do I contain their pain in the timetable of the day?

I am called to teach all the pupils in my class,
To stretch the minds of the brightest and the broken.
I need to meet so many needs that may never be spoken,
In the rough and tumble of the classroom.

Lord, be with me as I read the needs of my class.
The need to learn, to grow, to befriend and to celebrate.
Help me to know where I can make a difference,
What I can deal with in my role as a teacher,
And what I need to pass on to others.

Teach me to look at my pupils with gratitude,
See the hint of your presence in each of their faces.

Night Prayer before the Start of Term

The adrenalin is already in full flow!
Anxieties, questions, images and timetables
Are colliding in my mind like a major accident,
At the junction of this holiday and a new term.

I'm on the starting grid, taut and tense
Waiting for the alarm that will set me off
Into another term of teaching and learning,
In that whirlwind, called a school.

But here tonight, I'm wide awake but wanting to rest.
Like a rabbit in the headlights of an approaching term,
I am transfixed by the need to steel myself
For the change in pace and expectations of tomorrow.

As I lie awake, restless and filled with aimless anxiety,
Help me to remember other colleagues are doing the same.
Those same colleagues will arrive tomorrow,
Bleary eyed and edgy, for a new beginning.

It is part of the role of every teacher to manage anxiety,
To keep a focus on the enlivening of the young.
As I rest tonight Lord, help me to keep my focus
On things that will help me manage the first day back.

There will be friendly colleagues with energy to spare.
There will be stories of holidays and new patterns to begin.
Pupils will be fresh, rested and ready to work.
I will be glad to get started and use the energy I feel tonight.

So as I walk through the gate tomorrow morning Lord,
Be with me and keep me optimistic about this new beginning.
Let me allow others to be different and welcome changes
To styles, timetables and my own attitudes to work.

Stay with me in each class on my timetable,
Let me give them a clear lead for the rest of the term.
May I find time for listening and stories,
That will bridge the gap between holidays and term,
Between your presence and all those at school.

OTHER BOOKS BY DAVID O'MALLEY

ORDINARY WAYS
Spiritual reflections for teachers & youth
leaders

PRAYERS TO START THE DAY

PRAYERS TO CLOSE THE DAY

TRUST THE ROAD 2nd edition
with coloured illustrations

VIA LUCIS
The Stations of the Resurrection

More details and other resources can be obtained
from Don Bosco Publications.

www.don-bosco-publications.co.uk